Beyond
the Call
of Duty

BRAVERY IN
WORLD WAR I

WAYLAND

First published in 2013 by Wayland
Copyright © Wayland 2013

Wayland
338 Euston Road
London NW1 3BH

Wayland Australia
Level 17/207 Kent Street
Sydney, NSW 2000

Editor: Annabel Stones
Designer: Elaine Wilkinson
Researchers: Laura Simpson and Edward Field
at The National Archives

The National Archives looks after the UK government's historical documents. It holds records dating back nearly 1,000 years from the time of William the Conqueror's Domesday Book to the present day. All sorts of documents are stored there, including letters, photographs, maps and posters. They include great Kings and Queens, famous rebels like Guy Fawkes and the strange and unusual – such as reports of UFOs and even a mummified rat!

Material reproduced courtesy of The National Archives, London, England.
www.nationalarchives.gov.uk

Catalogue references and picture acknowledgements (Images from The National Archives unless otherwise stated): Cover (left photo) & p.15 (bottom left): AIR 1/169/15/160/5 24 Squadron, RFC and RAF, 1916; Cover (right photo) & Title page & p.7: RAIL 253/516 Postcard 1 of 2 from Pte H Giles November 1915; Cover (centre bottom photo) & p.13 (top): Wayland; Cover (right, medal): © Crown copyright 2013; p.2 & p.4 (bottom): RAIL 253/516 Royal Engineers Kirk, Boyce, Hodges, Bright, Robertson and Russell after joining, 1916; p.4 (top): RAIL 253/516 Royal Engineers Kirk, Boyce, Hodges, Bright, Robertson and Russell before joining, 1916; p.5 (middle): RAIL 343/753 (4) Troops travelling to Manchester for review by Lord Kitchener; p.5 (bottom): PRO 30/57/123 Your King and Country Need You poster 1914; p.6 (left), p.12 (left), p.20 (left) & p.26 (left): Shutterstock; p.7 (top left): WO 153/647 Mons, Le Cateau and the retreat August 1914; p.7 (top right): WO 98/8 Victoria Cross award for Lieutenant MJ Dease 1914; p.8 & p.19 (top): PRO 30/57/51/g3cs2s4 A series of photos showing the front line around the village of Loos, June 1915; p.9 (top): WO 297/2021 La Boutillerie; p.9 (top right): Shutterstock; p.10: WO 95/3911 3 Indian (Lahore) Division War Diary, Aug-Nov 1914; p.11 (top): Wayland; p.11 (bottom left) & p.30: Peter Hicks; p.13 (bottom): © Illustrated London News Ltd/ Mary Evans; p.14: RAIL 253/516 RFC group October 1916; p.15 (top right): AIR 1/724/91/7/ 29 Port view of one of the two RE8 prototypes, 7996 or 7997 [Reconnaissance Experimental] 28 June 1916; p.16: ADM 1/8331 The Navy Wants Men poster WWI; p.17 (top right): ADM 137/4825 1 of 5 German plan of Battle of Jutland 1916;

p.17 (bottom left): Peter Hicks; p.18: RAIL 253/ 516 Illustration of men in the trenches 1915-1918; p.19 (middle right): Shutterstock; p.21 (top): MUN 4/1085 Gun Ammunition (2) 1916; p.21 (bottom right): EXT 1/315 Learn To Make Munitions poster; p.22: WO 339/90293 Walter Tull Temporary Commission 5 December 1916; p.23 (top): IWM via Getty Images; p.23 (bottom left): Bruce Castle Museum (Haringey Culture, Libraries and Learning); p.24: WO 95/110 War Diary page 4 Brigade Tank Corps, 4 Battalion Tank Corps 1916 (10); p.25 (top): MUN 5/394 (22) Tank experiments 1915-1918; p.25 (bottom right): MUN 5/394 (74) Standard Mark IV tank 1914-1918; p.27 (top): WIKIMEDIA Stretcher_bearers_Battle_of_Thiepval_Ridge_ September_ 1916; p.27 (bottom right): Peter F Williams; p.28 (left): ADM 137/4710 German signal Battle of Jutland (1) 1916; p.28 (right): ADM 137/4710 German signal Battle of Jutland (5) 1916; p.29 (top): E 31/2/1 (162a) Domesday Book, Glos, Chepstow Castle (Striguil); p.29 (bottom): 800px-A_researcher_ working_with_delicate_resource_at_The_National_Archives.

Background images and other graphic elements courtesy of Shutterstock.

Please note:
The website addresses (URLs) included in this book were valid at the time of going to press. However, because of the nature of the Internet, it is possible that some addresses may have changed, or sites may have changed or closed down since publication. While the author and publishers regret any inconvenience this may cause to the readers, no responsibility for any such changes can be accepted by either the author or the publishers.

A cataloguing record for this title is available at the British Library.

ISBN 978 0 7502 7970 3

Dewey Number 940.4'00922

Printed in China

Wayland is a division of Hachette Children's Books, an Hachette UK company
www.hachette.co.uk

CONTENTS

WHAT IS BRAVERY?

What does the phrase 'beyond the call of duty' mean? Usually, it refers to a person who has gone further and achieved more than was expected of them. It is a quality that is often seen in life and death situations, when people are pushed to the limits of endurance.

In this book you will see examples of people who have shown astonishing courage. World War I was a hugely tragic event causing misery for millions. In spite of this, people often risked their own lives in order to save or help somebody else.

So, why do people do this? It is a very difficult question to answer, but we know that people do it all the time.

◀▲ Six friends who all joined the Royal Engineers together.

4

Governments have always acknowledged and decorated the brave of their country. Medals and ribbons have been awarded since the English Civil War (1642–51). They are an expression of thanks by the nation to someone who carries out a courageous or selfless act. They are also awarded to encourage and improve the morale of others. If a member of a regiment wins the Victoria Cross there is tremendous pride not only in the individual but also in the regiment itself.

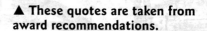

'I recommend his case as an acknowledgement of the high example set by him'

'courage and energy saved several lives... conspicuous gallantry and devotion to duty'

▲ These quotes are taken from award recommendations.

Sometimes awards are made for political reasons. Individuals are singled out and decorated as this can raise the population's morale. If bravery is celebrated a country can feel good about itself.

We must remember that people receiving decorations are not the only brave people. There were countless other examples of personal acts of heroism during World War I that were not witnessed or recorded. During difficult times both soldiers and civilians helped each other without thought of reward or praise.

▲ Troops travelling to Manchester for review by Lord Kitchener.

How it Began...

The causes of World War I (1914–18) are very complicated and historians still argue about them today. However, in the years leading up to 1914, the European powers were becoming more anxious. Germany, for example, was worried about being surrounded by France and Russia. After declaring war on her neighbours, Germany invaded Belgium in order to attack France. Britain, who supported Belgium, declared war on Germany on 4 August 1914.

▶ A 'Call to Arms' appealing to people's sense of duty to King and Country.

Your King & Country Need You.
A CALL to ARMS
An addition of **100,000** men to His Majesty's Regular Army is immediately necessary in the present grave National Emergency.
Lord Kitchener is confident that this appeal will be at once responded to by all those who have the safety of our Empire at heart.
Terms of Service.
General Service for a period of 3 years or until the war is concluded. Age of Enlistment between 19 and 30.
RATES OF PAY:
1s. 3d. to 10s. 6d. a day, according to Branch of Service and qualifications.
How to Join.
Full information can be obtained at
or any Post Office in the Kingdom or at any Military Depot.
GOD SAVE THE KING.

OPENING MOVES

In August 1914, the British Expeditionary Force (BEF) cautiously advanced from the Belgian coast, but failed to join up with their French allies. Based at the Belgian town of Mons, the BEF's five divisions waited for a German attack of... 38 divisions!

Name:
Lieutenant Maurice Dease and Private Sidney Godley

Ages: 24/25

Event: The Battle of Mons

Location: Belgium

Medals: Victoria Cross

Dates Awarded:
16/25 November 1914

The Mons-Condé Canal curls around Mons and it was here the BEF dug themselves in. Lieutenant Maurice Dease was in charge of 'C' Company of the Royal Fusiliers. The Germans were attacking from the north and would try to cross the canal. He set up two machine guns to protect the railway bridge across the canal. They could hear the German Army during the night, moving into the woods to the north of the canal.

On 23 August at 9 am the railway bridge was attacked. The machine gunners were wounded and had to be quickly replaced. Dease, directing operations near the bridge, tried to reach one of the guns but was wounded in the leg. Refusing treatment, he was hit again, but with his Sergeant he crawled to the middle of the bridge to try to reach the guns. They were both killed.

Then, Private Sidney Godley volunteered to man a gun, despite being under heavy gunfire. He continued firing to buy time for the rest of 'C' Company to retreat. To ensure the gun did not get into the hands of the enemy, Godley threw it into the canal. He then tried to retreat, but was taken prisoner.

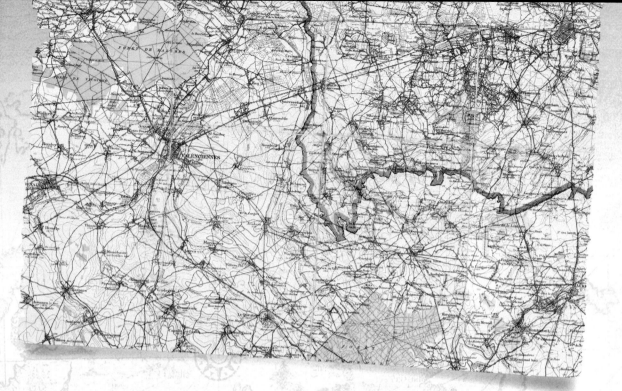

Hopelessly outnumbered, the BEF was ordered to withdraw. In the report of the event Dease's and Godley's exploits are recorded and both are recommended for a Victoria Cross. Their VCs were the first two awarded in World War I. Lt. Dease is buried in the nearby Symphorien Cemetery, where the very first and last fatalities of the war are buried.

▲ An early map of Mons, and the retreat of 1914.

A SECOND THOUGHT

Despite being wounded, why do you think Dease refused treatment?

Mons to Marne

The retreat from Mons allowed the BEF to join up with the French Army and they fought together at the Battle of the Marne in September 1914. This prevented the German Army from taking Paris and defeating France. For Germany, this meant their war plan – the Schlieffen Plan – had failed. The plan was to avoid fighting France and Russia at the same time. By failing to defeat France quickly, Germany had to fight on two fronts for most of the war.

▲ Soldiers were often billeted in tents when no buildings were available.

TRENCH RAID

By October 1914, the war of movement was over. Both sides had to dig in and, before long, a set of trenches faced each other, running from the North Sea to the Swiss border...

The reason soldiers lived in the trenches for nearly four years was because of the machine gun. Its murderous firepower meant soldiers had to live underground or be shot. The space between the two sets of trenches was called no man's land, because nobody owned it and if you ventured into it you risked death.

▼ A photograph looking over British and German trenches at Loos, near the French-Belgian border.

However, both sides organised raids on each other's trenches. Often they were beaten back, but when they were successful they gained a trench from the enemy. On 30 November 1914, Lieutenant Edward Shaw of the 1st Middlesex Regiment was ordered, with his platoon, to recover a trench that had been lost to the Germans at La Boutillerie in France.

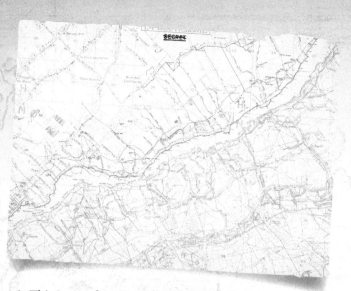

▲ This map of La Boutillerie shows the British (blue) and German (red) trenches.

The attack did not go well at first. Shaw was wounded and driven back with his men because of the ferocious German defence. He collected another party of men and tried again. This time, despite the rifle and machine gun fire, they got into the trench where Shaw was wounded for a second time. He and his men fought their way up the narrow trench and, after a fierce struggle, were able to recapture it and take many prisoners. For this action, in which he showed 'conspicuous gallantry', Shaw was awarded the Distinguished Service Order.

Shaw quickly recovered from his wounds and was soon back at the Front. He died from wounds he received in an attack at Les Boeufs on 7 December 1916.

A SECOND THOUGHT
If you were on a trench raid, would you prefer to try it at night or in daylight?

▲ Barbed wire was designed to stop or slow down soldiers, making them easier targets for machine gun or rifle fire.

Trench Warfare

The idea behind these raids was to enter the enemy's trench either by stealth or surprise. Lines of heavy barbed wire were designed to slow, snag or stop anyone approaching. This greatly increased the chance of detection and was probably the reason why Shaw's first attack failed. Trench warfare was always going to favour the defender. Every section of trench had a pair of heavy machine guns at each end that fired on attackers. This crossfire swept hundreds of bullets a minute across no man's land, so very few attackers ever stood a chance.

A LONG WAY FROM HOME

With the British Army fighting for survival in the early months of the war, it was decided to send two infantry divisions of the Indian Army to France. They reached Marseilles on 26 September and many arrived at the Western Front by the middle of October.

The Indian Army was made up of volunteers from the modern-day countries of India, Pakistan, Bangladesh and Nepal. The troops had to face worsening weather as heavy autumn rains were followed by a freezing, snowy winter. Despite the difficulties, the Indian Army quickly adapted to fighting in holes in the ground.

On 25 September at Fauquissart, near Neuve Chapelle in France, Rifleman Kulbir Thapa of the 3rd Gurkha Rifles was injured during a trench raid. While crawling back, he came across a wounded soldier from the Leicestershire Regiment, behind the German lines.

Kulbir stayed with the man all day and night, re-assuring him, tending to his wounds and trying to make him comfortable. When morning broke it was very misty and he used this cover to drag the soldier through the German barbed wire, leaving him safely in a shell hole.

▲ Trench diary showing the activities of the Jullundur Brigade.

'India Corps reported successful use of trench mortars today.'

An Empire Effort

The use of the Indian Army was a reminder that the British cause was supported by the Empire. Not only from India, but troops from Australia, South Africa, the West Indies and other British colonies all contributed to the war effort. The Indian Army played a crucial part in 'holding the line' during 1914–15 because of shortages of British troops. They were withdrawn from France in October 1915.

▲ Indian troops march down from the mountains.

Incredibly, Kulbir then went back for two fellow wounded Gurkhas he had seen in no man's land and carried them to safety one at a time.

Then, in broad daylight and under fire, he returned to the shell hole where he had left the wounded soldier and carried him back to the British trenches. Some accounts say that watching German soldiers clapped and encouraged Kulbir, they were so impressed by his actions!

Officers witnessed this action and Kulbir was recommended for the Victoria Cross. The story even reached King George V who was also impressed. Kulbir was invited to Buckingham Palace and his 'King Emperor' presented him personally with his medal.

▲ The Chattri is a memorial to the Indian soldiers who fought in World War I.

A SECOND THOUGHT

Indian troops fought in a war thousands of miles away from their home. How would this make you feel?

FRONT-LINE NURSES

Traditionally in wartime, women were not allowed within five kilometres of the front-line fighting. Mairi Chisholm and Elsie Knocker decided that was not near enough...

Name:
Mairi Chisholm
and Elsie Knocker

Age: 25/30

Location: Belgium

Medals:
Military Medal/Order of
St. John of Jerusalem

Date Awarded:
1917/ 27 October 1927

When asked if she would like to help wounded soldiers in war-torn Belgium, Mairi Chisholm accepted gladly. She was paired with a trained nurse – Elsie Knocker – and they travelled to the war zone in September 1914.

Elsie noticed the high number of soldiers dying in transit and suggested setting up a first aid post close to the trenches where casualties could be treated before evacuation to the hospitals. They set up a British first aid post in the ruined village of Pervyse. It was a small cellar, just two metres square, and only 100 metres from the front line. The water supply was contaminated and even after boiling tasted revolting!

Elsie carried out the specialist first aid, while Mairi was the main ambulance driver and mechanic. On freezing nights she took soup and cocoa to the shivering soldiers in the trenches.

The cellar was not fit for purpose – they had trouble getting stretchers in and out – so they moved to a bigger house further away from the front line. As well as the wounded, they helped soldiers suffering from the unpleasantness of trench life – trench foot, infected cuts, painful boils, trench fever and sores. By 1915 they had so impressed the authorities that they were allowed to stay permanently. They became celebrities and newspapers called them the Heroines of Pervyse. That year, King Albert of Belgium honoured them with the Star of the Order of Leopold and more awards followed.

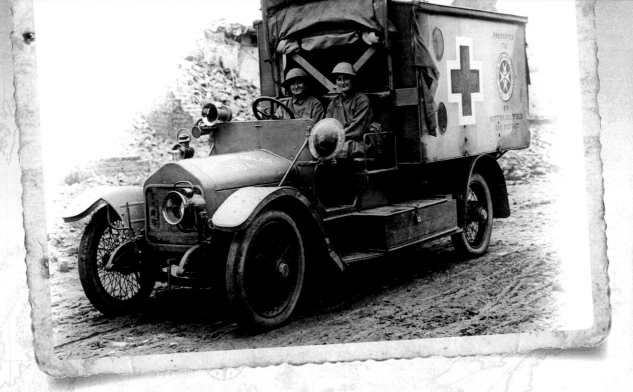

▲ Mairi Chisholm and Elsie Knocker driving their ambulance through the ruins of northern Belgium.

They carried on their exceptional work until March 1918, when both were caught in a gas attack – Elsie severely. Mairi recovered, but on returning suffered a more serious gas attack. She returned to Britain, where they both finished the war in the Women's Royal Air Force.

A SECOND THOUGHT
There were many dangers when working so close to the front line. What would you have worried about?

Medical Organisation

Marie's and Elsie's work highlighted the poor medical organisation in 1914. Very soon the Royal Army Medical Corps organised the collection, evacuation and distribution of casualties. A triage system was introduced and is still used in hospitals today. With this, the wounded were graded according to the seriousness of their injuries. Many men still died of relatively minor wounds. This was because they became seriously infected at a time when antibiotics were not available.

▲ A dressing station on the Western Front.

THE WAR IN THE AIR

The Royal Flying Corps (RFC) was the air arm of the British Army from 1912 to 1918. From August 1914 it supported troops on the ground with spying missions and even light bombing raids, but it was to become more important...

Name:
Lieutenant Frederick Powell
Age: 20
Location:
The Western Front
Event: War in the air
Medal: Military Cross
Date Awarded:
14 January 1916

In 1914 Frederick Powell was desperate to get to the war. But he was stuck in an army infantry regiment in England with no prospect of getting to France. One day he replied to an advert from the Royal Flying Corps (RFC) looking for volunteer observers. He was successful but it turned out there were too many observers and men were being sent back to England.

So Powell volunteered as a pilot and was accepted. He received his Royal Aero Club flying certificate on 2 March 1915.

Powell's flying career did not start very well. Showing off in front of his comrades, he attempted a loop from a standing start. The plane crashed and he was lucky to escape with his life. He gradually improved

▶ As well as pilots, RFC squadron included important technical support from fitters, riggers and armourers.

as a pilot and in September 1915 claimed his first victory. He shot down an enemy plane in his Vickers 'Gunbus' plane.

On 2 January 1916 he and his observer were flying a normal patrol when suddenly they were surprised by an enormous plane – 'Two-Tails' as they were called. He shouted to his observer to point his gun upwards and fire while Powell flew underneath. The enemy plane went down in a spiral and crashed behind enemy lines. A week later Powell was awarded the Military Cross.

In his career, Powell had six confirmed and nine possible victories. On 2 February 1918 he was shot down, survived and held prisoner until the end of the war.

▲ The RE8, known as the 'Harry Tate'. Over 4,000 saw service on the Western Front.

Aeroplanes become Weapons

With the stalemate of trench warfare, the role of the Royal Flying Corps increased. Their planes had cameras mounted on the sides and they were expected to carry out photographic reconnaissance of enemy trench systems. With so much traffic in the air, both sides also mounted guns and fired at each other. The aeroplane had become a weapon in its own right. Heavier planes were able to carry high explosive bombs and both sides targeted crowds of troops, airfields, stores and ammunition dumps. These attacks were very hit-and-miss until a simple bomb aimer was invented in 1915.

▲ The Vickers FB5 fighter, known as the 'Gunbus'. It usually had a Lewis machine gun mounted at the front.

A SECOND THOUGHT
Why do think the troops in the trenches might have resented RFC pilots?

THE WAR AT SEA

The British Grand Fleet and the German High Seas Fleet were the world's biggest navies in 1914. When war broke out, Britain's Navy was used to block essential war supplies from reaching Germany. Would the two fleets ever meet in battle?

Name:
John 'Jack' Cornwell

Age: 16

Location: The North Sea

Event:
The Battle of Jutland

Medal: Victoria Cross

Date Awarded:
15 September 1916

THE NAVY WANTS MEN

Recruits required at once for
**R.N.V.R.
SIGNAL BRANCH**
INCLUDING WIRELESS TELEGRAPHY.

QUALIFICATIONS:
AGE: 17 years and 6 months to 22 years.
EDUCATION: Not below an seventh standard, Good Writing and Spelling.
Good Eyesight and Hearing.

PAY FROM 1/3 A DAY
And Separation Allowance.

APPLY:
Naval Recruiting Office,
Great Scotland Yard, S.W. 1.

▲ Recruitment for the Navy. RNVR stands for Royal Naval Volunteer Reserve.

On 31 May 1916 the German Fleet under Admiral Scheer put to sea for a sweep along the Danish coast. The British Fleet under Admiral Jellicoe, knowing the Germans were in the North Sea, also set sail for the same destination.

On board HMS *Chester*, one of the British Light Cruisers, was Boy Seaman First Class, 16-year-old John 'Jack' Cornwell. He had given up his job as a delivery boy in east London and joined the Navy without his father's permission. He was trained as a sight-setter on naval guns and had joined the HMS *Chester* in April 1916.

On 31 May, his ship was scouting ahead for its battleship squadron when it became aware of distant gunfire. At 5.30 pm it came under tremendous fire from German cruisers. 17 shells hit *Chester* in quick succession and Jack's gun was badly damaged.

The Battle of Jutland

The attack on HMS *Chester* marked the start of the Battle of Jutland. This was the biggest battle of World War I and both sides claimed victory. Although the German fleet sunk more tonnage of ships than the British, after the battle the German High Seas Fleet retreated to their naval base until the end of the war. The battle was named 'Jutland' because it was fought in the North Sea just west of the 'Jutland' peninsula of Denmark.

Schauplatz der Seeschlacht am 31. Mai 1916

▲ The scene of the Battle of Jutland.

The ship's gun shields did not reach the deck so shell splinters badly injured the legs of the gunners. All the crew were killed except Jack who, although terribly injured, remained standing for more than 15 minutes, his eyes on the gun-sights, waiting for orders.

When medical orderlies reached him they took him below deck, while the damaged HMS *Chester* retired from the battle. Reaching the port of Immingham, Jack was transferred to hospital where he died from his wounds on 2 June.

Three months later the Admiralty decided to honour the boy sailor with the highest medal for bravery. Jack Cornwell was posthumously awarded the Victoria Cross. His recommendation reads: 'devotion to duty...standing alone at a most exposed post, quietly awaiting orders till the end of the action...I recommend his case as an acknowledgement of the high example set by him'.

▲ The boy sailor, John 'Jack' Cornwell's grave at Manor Park, east London.

A SECOND THOUGHT

Why do you think Jack did not tell his father he was joining the Navy?

TRENCH WARFARE

The soldiers of World War I had a love-hate relationship with the trenches they lived, worked and fought in. On the one hand, the trenches protected them from bullets and shell fragments; on the other they were dirty, smelly, wet and dangerous places.

Name: Company Sergeant Major H.C. Wright

Location: Western Front

Medal:
Mentioned in Despatches / Distinguished Conduct Medal

Date Awarded:
13 February 1917/
1 January 1918

Trenches were simple excavations in the ground. Protection could be increased by making piles of earth at the front and back of the trench as well as with sandbags. The main problem was that they attracted water. France and Belgium have lots of rain, especially in winter. When the rain saturated the earth it became soft and the trenches often collapsed.

Sergeant H.C. Wright of the East Kent Regiment was very good at his job, so much so that by January 1917 he was Acting Company Sergeant Major. He was responsible for discipline, standards and distribution of ammunition in the Company, as well as evacuating the wounded and collecting prisoners of war. In February,

he was 'Mentioned in Despatches' and praised for his 'cheerfulness...great energy' and always 'set a splendid example to the men'.

By September 1917, Wright was promoted to full Company Sergeant Major and was clearly liked and respected by all.

▶ A cheery Christmas card from the trenches. In reality it was a lot less comfortable.

▲ The German front line seen from the British sector.

In December that year, a German shell landed in the soft earth and exploded. Part of the trench and a dugout caved in, burying many men alive. Gas shells also burst near the trench filling the air and ground with fumes. Without waiting to put on his gas mask, Wright dug furiously with his bare hands to try to reach the trapped men. The sodden earth, reeking with poisonous gas was lethal. He pulled out three men, but was badly affected by the gas himself. He carried on digging and refused to leave the rescue until ordered to by an officer.

Wright's courage and energy saved several lives. He was awarded the Distinguished Conduct Medal for 'conspicuous gallantry and devotion to duty'.

▲ Front-line troops with respirators during a gas alert.

Gas Attack!

Poison gas was first used by the Germans at the 2nd Battle of Ypres in April 1915. By the end of the year, both sides were using it. Gas caused death, and more often permanent damage and suffering for those caught without a gas mask. Changes in wind direction was its main weakness, so gas 'shells' were invented that dropped accurately into and around trench lines. Both sides would have increased the use of gas shells, had the war not ended.

A SECOND THOUGHT
How do you think damp, muddy trenches affected the morale of front-line troops?

WAR WORKERS

The guns of the British Army had a greedy need for millions of shells. Munitions factories opened up all over Britain and sometimes they were as dangerous as the Front Line....

Names:
Mabel Lethbridge

Age: 17

Location: Hayes, London

Event:
Munitions explosion

Medal:
Order of the British Empire

Date Awarded:
1 January 1918

Mabel Lethbridge volunteered to work at the Hayes Munitions Factory, London, when she was 17. But, she told officials there that she was 18, and she told her mother she was sewing aircraft wings.

After a few days in the factory she volunteered for the Danger Zone where ancient 'monkey machines' forced highly explosive amatol into 18-pound shell cases. The girls pulled a rope to raise a heavy weight (the 'beater') and dropped it on to the amatol to pack it tight and allow room for the fuses. It was very physical and dangerous work and Mabel went home aching and exhausted. Everyone knew the old machines were dangerous. The new ones had been delivered but not yet installed.

During one shift – just before 3pm – her friend said 'Last shell'. Then, there was a massive explosion, a flash, a deafening roar and Mabel was hurled through the air. The hut became a blazing furnace. She was aware of a voice shouting, 'Mabel crawl! For God's sake crawl!' Mabel lost her left leg, was operated on for 13 life-threatening injuries and was temporarily blinded. She clung to life, but all her friends were dead...

On recovering, Mabel's family had a terrible fight with the authorities over compensation. Girls under 18 years-of-age were not allowed in the Danger Zone. She was not entitled to a pension and under the Worker's Compensation Act she received £1 per week. She had worked only nine days in the factory but her accident was the start of years of financial difficulty.

▲ Women 'munitioneers'. These huge factories were very dangerous places to work.

Mabel received hundreds of letters of support. One even came from Buckingham Palace; it awarded her the Most Excellent Order of the British Empire, 'for courage and high example shown on the occasion of an explosion during which she lost a leg and sustained severe injuries'.
(1 January 1918)

A SECOND THOUGHT
Why do you think Mabel volunteered for the Danger Zone?

Munitions Factories

The women who kept the guns firing faced many dangers. Their skin often turned yellow because of the sulphur and many developed stomach cramps, sickness and constipation from the chemicals. Every day, they were given a pint of milk to 'neutralise' these poisonous substances. The biggest dangers were the explosions which were very common. In Faversham, Kent, in 1916 an explosion in a shell factory killed 105 people. A year later at Silvertown in West Ham, 73 were killed and 400 injured. At Chilwell, just outside Nottingham, in July 1918, a factory blew up, killing 134 and injuring 250.

THESE WOMEN ARE DOING THEIR BIT

LEARN TO MAKE MUNITIONS

▲ A propaganda poster to encourage more women into war work.

WALTER TULL
– UNRECOGNISED HERO

The extraordinary story of Walter Tull, professional footballer and the first black officer in the British Army, is a good example of how acts of courage can go unrecognised...

▲ Walter Tull's application to become an officer (known as gaining a commission).

Walter Tull was a talented professional footballer who played for Tottenham Hotspur and Northampton Town. When the war broke out, he volunteered for the Football Battalion (17th Middlesex Regiment).

Walter thrived in the army and gained promotion. As a Lance-Sergeant in Northern France, he served in the front line but was diagnosed with 'acute mania' – also called shell shock – caused by the massive artillery barrages that exploded in and around the trenches. After recovering, he returned to France and fought in the last weeks of the horrendous Battle of the Somme. Following this, Lieutenant-Colonel Browne recommended him for an officer's commission. He must have been really impressed because Military Law forbade anyone not of pure European descent becoming an officer, and Tull's father was from Barbados.

22

Spring Offensive

The Spring Offensive of March 1918 was the last attempt by the Germans to win the war. The aim was to break the line of the British 5th Army with waves of attacking German soldiers. It pushed the British back, and broke the line in places, but ran out of momentum. The Germans tried again in April and again in May, but each attack was weaker than the previous. The British, now supported by American troops in France, held the line and in August forced the German Army to retreat.

▲ The Royal Field Artillery in action during the Spring Offensive.

Nevertheless, Tull did his officer training and passed on 19 May 1917. He had become Britain's first black officer.

Tull fought in the Battle of Passchendaele, and in November was sent to fight in Italy. He led his men on a number of dangerous raids, including an important one on 1 January 1918. Major-General Lawson personally congratulated Tull on his 'gallantry and coolness' in leading the raid and not losing any casualties despite heavy enemy fire.

Tull arrived back in France on 8 March. About a fortnight later, the Germans launched their massive Spring Offensive. Tull helped his men retreat but on 25 March, he was hit by a machine gun bullet and killed. Private Tom Billingham tried to recover his body, but the German troops were so close he had to leave it. Tull's body was never found.

A SECOND THOUGHT

Although Walter Tull was recommended for the Military Cross, he never received it. There is a campaign to get Walter Tull awarded a posthumous Military Cross. What do you think should happen?

▲ Walter in his full Tottenham Hotspur kit at White Hart Lane.

TANK AGAINST TANK

During the war on the Western Front, both sides tried to introduce weapons that would break the deadlock. The British used the tank in 1916, but the first tank battle did not take place until April 1918.

Name:
Lieutenant Frank Mitchell

Location:
Western Front, France

Event:
World's first tank battle

Medal:
Military Cross

Date Awarded:
16 September 1918

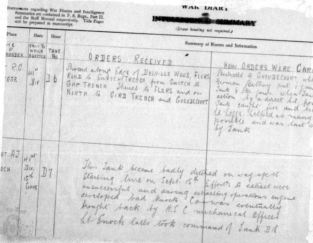

▲ **Extract from a Tank diary. Tank D7 broke down near Delville Wood on the Somme.**

The tank was the great hope of the British Army on the Western Front. With thick armour and a range of guns it could smash its way through defences and give cover to advancing infantry.

Lieutenant Frank Mitchell was commander of a Mark IV tank during the Spring Offensive of April 1918. On 23 April, his job was to push forward with two other Mark IVs and join up with the British infantry. Suddenly, he saw a group of three, squat, tortoise-like German Av7 tanks. Mitchell realised he was about to engage his rivals at last – in the first ever tank battle!

His crew zig-zagged the tank into the space between trenches and were able to fire twice from their 6-pounder guns. The Germans delayed, but they then fired back armour-piercing bullets. Steel fragments shot all over the cab and the crew dived to the floor, but the machine-gunner was wounded in the legs by the bullets.

▲ This Mark IV tank is similar to Frank Mitchell's.

By now the Mark IV was entering shell holes and the up-and-down motion made accurate firing difficult. Stopping, they fired at the leading German tank and hit the turret, knocking it out. Mitchell fired on the two other tanks and they both retreated.

German artillery and planes were now trying to stop the British tank. The crew recovered, but nearly tipped over into a huge shell hole. A fourth German tank appeared and they exchanged shots. Then, there was a loud 'crack' and Mitchell's tank drove round in circles. The artillery had destroyed one of their caterpillar tracks. The battle was over and the men retreated, with the injured, to their own lines.

A SECOND THOUGHT

Knowing the terrible conditions inside them, why do you think men volunteered to work in the new tanks?

Tank Troubles

In reality the tank was slow and kept breaking down. It had poor visibility, communication and terrible conditions for the crew – poisonous fumes, stifling heat and the risk of fire. The Mark IV was a huge improvement and Britain's most important tank in the war. Tanks played a major role in the breakthrough of the German lines on 8 August 1918, when Australian and Canadian troops advanced 12 kilometres into the German lines.

▲ A Mark IV tank.

STRETCHER-BEARER

Some of the bravest men in the war were the stretcher-bearers. They were not armed and their job was to comb the Collecting Zone, which usually meant no man's land, to pick up the badly wounded.

Name: Ernest Corey

Age: 25

Location: Western Front, France/Belgium

Medal:
Military Medal and 3 Bars

Date Awarded:
5 June, 10 November 1917;
8 September,
3 October 1918

Corey was a member of the Australian 55th Battalion, grenade section, and arrived in France in 1917. During a battle at Queant, near Cambrai, France, casualties were so high that his Commanding Officer asked for volunteer stretcher-bearers. Corey stepped forward and for the next 17 hours he carried the wounded over a kilometre to the Regimental Aid Post (RAP). Corey was awarded the Military Medal for his courageous actions.

Corey became a regular stretcher-bearer, he learned basic first aid and served in the battle of Polygon Wood in September 1917. This was part of the larger Battle of Passchendaele,

one of the worst battles of the whole conflict. Under intense machine gun and artillery fire he ventured into no man's land many times to help and collect the wounded. He was then awarded a bar to his Military Medal (which means he was awarded it again!).

After leave in Britain he returned to the Front just in time for the 'big push' against the German positions on the Somme in August 1918. In the capture of Peronne, Corey's bravery was again extraordinary and despite deadly artillery barrages he was able to greatly relieve the sufferings of the men and carried them to safety. For this he was awarded a second bar to his Military Medal!

Stretcher-bearers

The large number of casualties caused by modern weapons meant that stretcher-bearers were incredibly valuable servicemen on the battlefield. However, each company only had four stretcher-bearers and during battle this was not enough. Being a stretcher-bearer was incredibly difficult and tiring. Carrying a man on a stretcher through thick mud, while trying to keep him comfortable, was exhausting.

▲ Stretcher-bearers were very exposed and vulnerable to injury during artillery attacks in the trenches.

Now a corporal, Corey was put in charge of all the Battalion's stretcher-bearers. On 30 September, near Bullecourt, while in the thick of the fighting, Corey was badly injured in his right leg. He needed two operations and was discharged from the Army in June 1919. For his 'courage, coolness and devotion' at Bellecourt, he was awarded a third bar to his Military Medal, which is a record!

▶ The memorial to Ernest Corey at Cooma, New South Wales, Australia.

A SECOND THOUGHT

Why do you think some men preferred to be stretcher-bearers rather than fight in the trenches?

RESEARCH AND RECORDS

You have learned about some exceptional people in this book. How, in circumstances of great danger, they showed supreme levels of courage and great strength of character. So, how do we know that Lt. Maurice Dease tried to stop the Germans at Mons? Where is the evidence that Mabel Lethbridge applied to work in the Danger Zone? Where is the documentation that Ernest Corey gained three bars to his Military Medal?

When historians write about the past they use documents that give evidence about what happened many years ago. Just like a detective, they will look for written, visual and spoken clues about the past. If they wanted to research the Battle of Jutland (see page 17) they would look at official government and naval documents, film and photographic evidence and personal writings like diaries and letters.

◀ **Notes of a German signal from the Battle of Jutland.**

So, where is evidence like this kept? Documents are stored in an archive. They come in all sizes from small local ones to large national archives. The National Archives at Kew is one of the biggest in the world and it contains millions of files going back over 1000 years! They even have the Domesday Book – an amazingly detailed survey of England commissioned by William the Conqueror in 1086.

▲ Entry in the Domesday Book for Chepstow Castle.

The National Archives preserves important government papers and files, photographs, posters, maps, plans, drawings and paintings. They even have electronic records and digital files.

Pieces of paper that are the raw material of history can tell you things you expect, but they also tell you unusual things. For example, a government file might tell you what was decided about conscripting men into the armed forces in 1916, but it might also hint at the arguments between ministers in coming to the decision. Historians call this 'witting' and 'unwitting' testimony.

◄ A researcher at The National Archives looks carefully through incredibly old material.

GLOSSARY

Av7 – A type of German tank.

bar – When a medal has been awarded again.

BEF – British Expeditionary Force. The British Army in France and Belgium 1914–18.

blockade – When imports and exports are prevented going in and out of a country.

company – A military unit of the British Army of 227 men, made up of four platoons.

conscription – When a person is called up for compulsory military service.

division – A military unit of the British Army of about 18,000 men.

infantry – Soldiers who fight on foot.

in transit – Being moved e.g. in an ambulance.

Mentioned in Despatches – A person mentioned in a report by a senior officer for showing gallantry.

platoon – A military unit of the British Army of 52 men.

posthumously – Meaning after death. Such as a decoration being awarded after a person's death.

private – Lowest level of rank in the military.

RAP – Regimental Aid Post, where wounded soldiers were first taken.

reconnaissance – Spying on enemy land to get information.

sandbags – A small sack filled with earth or sand, used to strengthen trench defences.

Spring Offensive – The last attempt by the German Army to win the war, March–May, 1918.

trench fever – An infection spread by lice bites.

trench foot – A serious infection caused by wet and cold conditions.

triage – Organising and treating wounded soldiers according to the severity of their injuries.

Western Front – A zone of fighting in World War I in Western Europe.

FURTHER INFORMATION

BOOKS

Men, Women and Children in The First World War
by Phillip Steele, Wayland (2013)

Private Peaceful
by Michael Morpurgo, Harper Collins Children's Books (2004)

The First World War 1914–1918
by Pam Robson, Wayland (2013)

War in the Trenches: Remembering World War I
by Peter Hicks, Wayland (2013)

WEBSITES

www.nationalarchives.gov.uk
Website of The National Archives

www.nationalarchives.gov.uk/education/greatwar/
The National Archives' educational page for World War I.

www.bbc.co.uk/schools/worldwarone/
BBC history site with stories from World War I.

www.spartacus.schoolnet.co.uk/FWW.htm
Lots of information about World War 1 with a section on war heroes.

INDEX

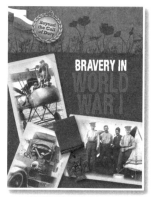

9780750279703

9780750279734

9780750279710

9780750279727

CONTENTS OF TITLES IN THE SERIES

BRAVERY IN WORLD WAR I

What is Bravery?
Opening Moves
Trench Raid
A Long Way From Home
Front-line Nurses
The War in the Air
The War at Sea
Trench Warfare
War Workers
Walter Tull – Unrecognised Hero
Tank Against Tank
Stretcher Bearer
Research and Records

BRAVERY IN WORLD WAR II

What is Bravery?
Dunkirk Evacuation
The Battle of Britain
Blitz!
Dam Busters
Women's War Work
Atlantic Convoys
Special Operations
Commando Raid
The Great Escape
Behind Enemy Lines
D-Day
Research and Records

CIVILIAN BRAVERY IN THE WORLD WARS

What is Bravery?
Trapped Behind Enemy Lines
The Lady on the Black Horse
Death from the Sky
An Awful Splendour
Legion d'Honneur
Blitz
Firefighter
Shark-infested Waters
Hull Had No Peace
Ammunition Train
Beyond Human Endurance
Research and Records

ANIMAL BRAVERY IN WARTIME

What is Bravery?
Dog Training School
Patrols and Parachutes
Horses at the Front
A Lucky Charm
Small Bird, Big Heart
Special Agent Pigeon
The Other War Horses
Gallantry on all Fronts
The Heavy Brigade
The Soldier Bear
One of the Family
Research and Records